Learning about...

First published in 1995 by Editiones Este, S.A.
Text: Josep M. Fité
Illustrations: Luis Rizo

Realización: Ediciones Este, S.A.
Director Editorial: Josep M. Parramón Homs
Editor: Isidro Sánchez

© Ediciones Este, S.A., 1995.

Fotocomposición y fotomecánica: Fimar, S.A.
Barcelona (España)

Impreso en España

First published in 1998 in the United States by
 Silver Press
A Division of Simon & Schuster
299 Jefferson Road, Parsippany, NJ 07054

Library of Congress Cataloging-in-Publication Data
Fité, Josep M.
[Yo aprendo a contar. English]
Learning about counting/by Josep M. Fité.
p. cm. (Mathematics for children)
Includes index.
Summary: Illustrations present the numbers from one to ten,
accompanied by simple problems involving counting,
addition, and subtraction.
1. Arithmetic—Juvenile literature. 2. Counting—Juvenile
literature. [1. Counting. 2. Arithmetic.] I. Rizo, Luis, ill.
II. Title. III. Series: Fité, Josep M. Mathematics for
children.
QA115.F5813   1997   96-36813
513.2'11—dc   CIP   AC

[E]

ISBN 0-382-39878-5 (LSB)   1 2 3 4 5 6 7 8 9 10
ISBN 0-382-39879-3 (pbk)   1 2 3 4 5 6 7 8 9 10

Mathematics for Children

Learning About

Counting

Silver Press
Parsippany, New Jersey

What are numbers?

The numbers are:

1 2 3 4 5 6 7 8 9

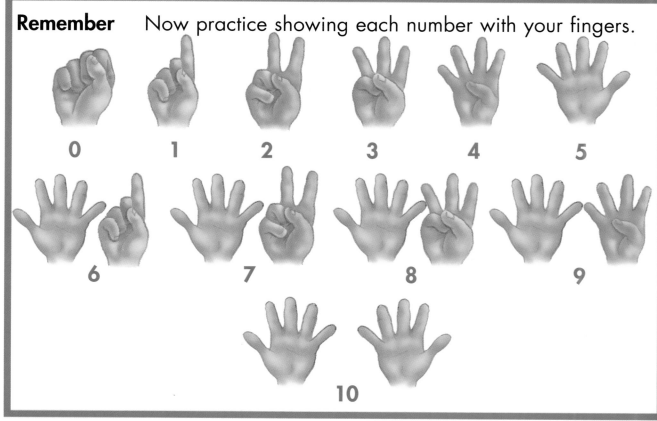

Remember   Now practice showing each number with your fingers.

0   1   2   3   4   5

6   7   8   9

10

Try this

Look at the shape of the pine tree. What number does it look like?

Look

A pine tree has a shape like the number 4. The chair does too. Look around for other objects with shapes like numbers. A pair of eyeglasses could be a number 8.

How many numbers do you see?

Do you know these number names? Can you say them?

10	11	12	20	21	22
ten	eleven	twelve	twenty	twenty-one	twenty-two

Try to say the numbers on the clock.

Remember If you write 1 and 2 next to each other, you make 12. If you write 2 and 2 next to each other, you make 22.

Try this

Look for the numbers in the picture.
Can you say them?

Look

- What numbers are
  in your address?

- What year were
  you born?

What do we do when we count?

When we count, we find out how many of something there are.

1 one

2 two

3 three

Remember
1 **2** **3** **4** **5** **6**

Try this

Count the snails, the mushrooms, and the trees in this picture.

Now count the leaves. Draw two more on a piece of paper.

Count on your own.

How many people are there in the family in the picture? How many people are in your family?

What do we count with?

We count with numbers.

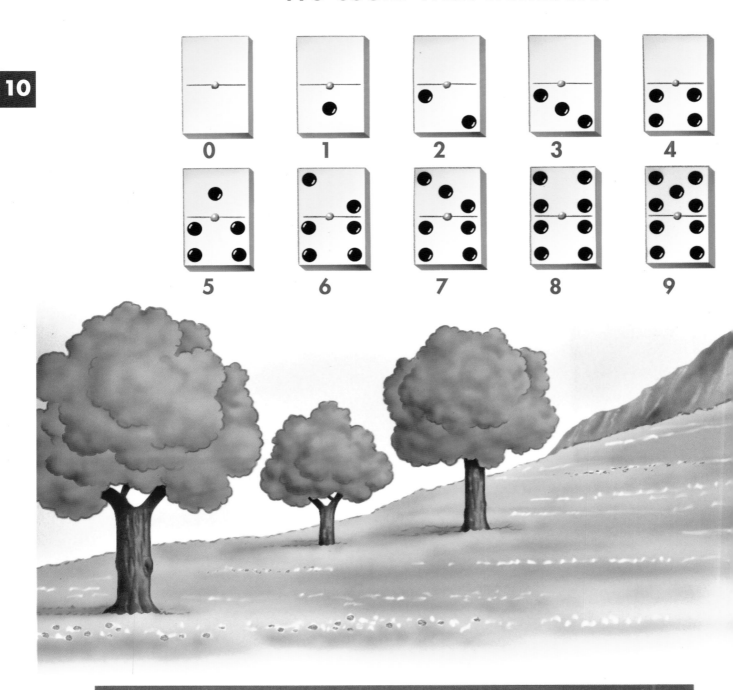

0   1   2   3   4

5   6   7   8   9

Remember

Anytime you see you write 3

Try this

In this picture, there is/are

One (1)	sun	Two (2)	?
Three (3)	?	Four (4)	?

Count on your own.

How many pencils
are there?

Count the balls.
Then write the number.

What do we need counting for?

We need to count to find out how many things there are.

2 birds
two

1 tree
one

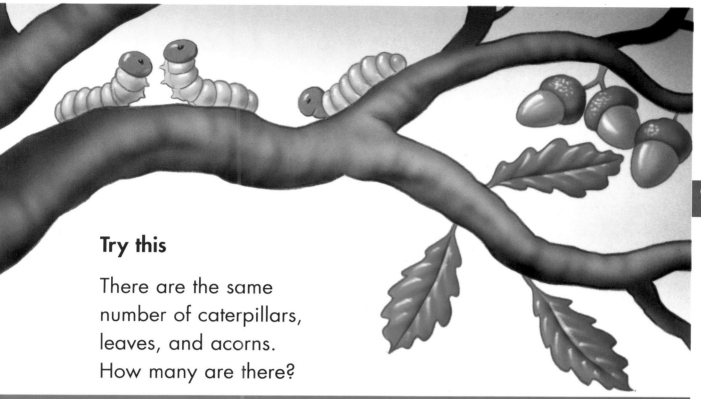

Try this

There are the same
number of caterpillars,
leaves, and acorns.
How many are there?

Count on your own.

- Count the girls
- Count the tables
- Count the boys
- Count the chairs.
- Count the school bags.

How do we count?

We count by grouping things.

one

two

three

four

five

six

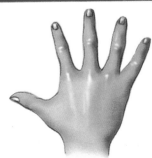

Remember

Make groups of things. Then count.
How many fingers do you see?

Try this

How many beach umbrellas do you see?
How many pails? How many shovels?

Count on your own.

How many days are there in a week?

Monday	Tuesday	Wednesday	Thursday
Friday	Saturday	Sunday	Count them!

What is addition?

Addition means to know how many things you have by joining groups.

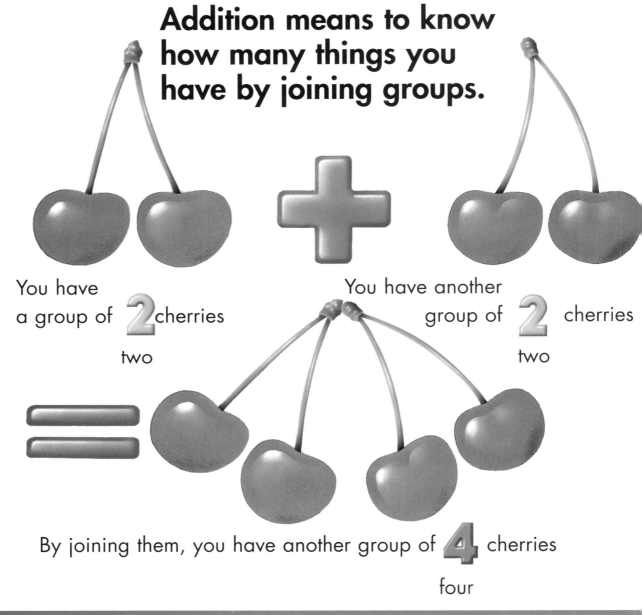

You have a group of **2** cherries
two

You have another group of **2** cherries
two

By joining them, you have another group of **4** cherries
four

Count the cherries.

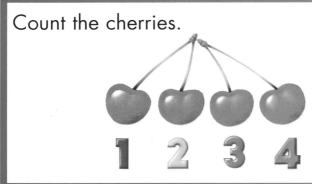

1 2 3 4

Remember
If you count the cherries, the total is 4. If you use addition, the answer is the same.

Try this

How many red fish?

And how many yellow fish?

How many fish all together? Add the red fish and the yellow fish.

Add on your own.
You have 4 red buttons and 2 yellow buttons.

Add them to find out how many buttons you have all together.

What do we use to add?

We add with things or with groups of things.

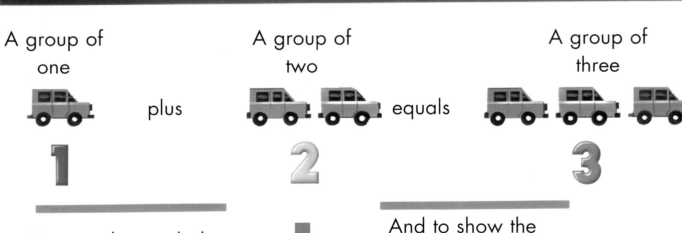

A group of one

plus

A group of two

equals

A group of three

1

2

3

You use this symbol when you add:

+

And to show the total you use this symbol:

=

Remember

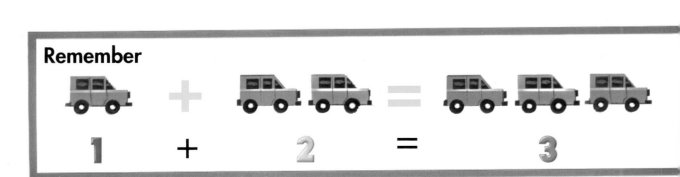

1   +   2   =   3

Try this

There are two giraffes and four elephants in the picture.
Use the correct symbols you need to add.

 ☐  ☐

Add on your own

Write on a piece of
paper the numbers
and the symbols to
show the total number
of animals.

What do we need addition for?

Addition helps us so we do not have to count one by one every time.

When you want to buy something, you know what coins to use.

How many coins do you need to buy a bag of candies?

Remember

1 + 1 = 2	4 + 1 = 5	7 + 1 = 8
2 + 1 = 3	5 + 1 = 6	8 + 1 = 9
3 + 1 = 4	6 + 1 = 7	

Try this

If the toy truck costs 9 pennies, how many coins would you need to buy it? How many coins would you need to buy the ball? the train? the car? the teddy bear?

Add on your own

Look at the box. How many pencils are there? How many erasers? How many sharpeners? When you finish counting, add them all together.

How do we add?

We add by joining things in order to make bigger groups.

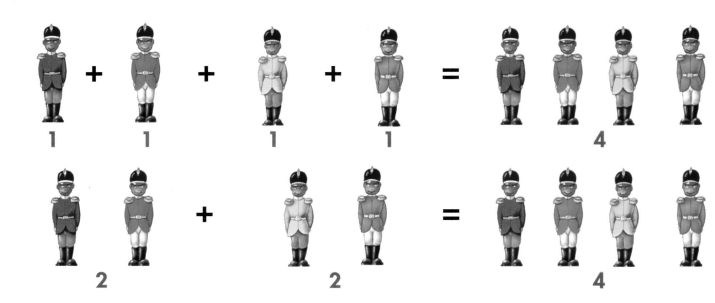

You can also add different things:

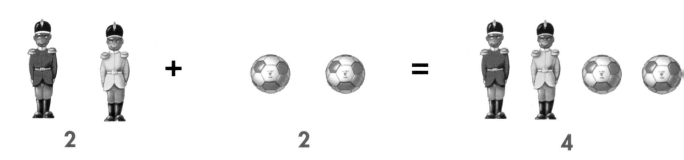

Remember		
1 + 2 = 3	4 + 2 = 6	7 + 2 = 9
2 + 2 = 4	5 + 2 = 7	
3 + 2 = 5	6 + 2 = 8	

Try this

Add the oranges and the tomatoes. Add the melon and the apples.
By adding you can make groups of different things.

Add on your own

Look at the toy box. Count the
toy cars and the balls. Add the
two groups. Also add the story
books. How many all together?

What is subtraction?

Subtraction is the taking away of a group of things from another group of things.

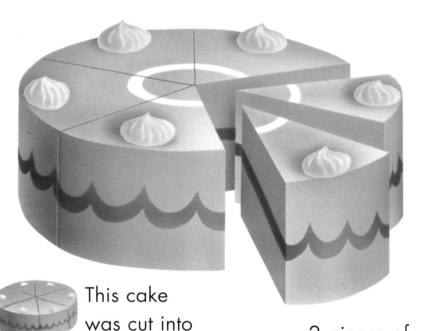

This cake was cut into 6 pieces.

4 pieces are left.

2 pieces of cake have been cut and taken away.

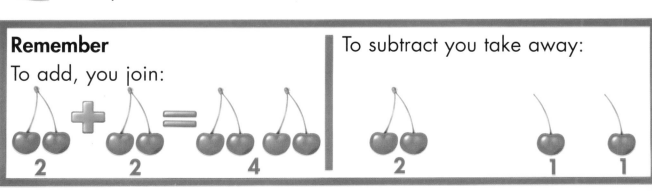

Remember

To add, you join:

2 + 2 = 4

To subtract you take away:

2   1   1

Try this

- How many balloons all together?
- How many balloons is the man holding?
- How many balloons did he let go?

Subtract on your own.

How many pages does this book have? How many pages have you read? How many pages do you still have to read?

You got all these gifts for your birthday. If you open the ones with the bows first, how many other gifts do you still have to open?

What do we need to subtract?

We subtract with things or groups of things.

A group of **5**

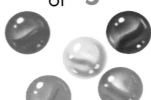

we subtract

Take away a group of **3**

we keep

We have a group of **2**

To show subtraction we use this symbol:

And to show the result, we use this symbol:

Remember

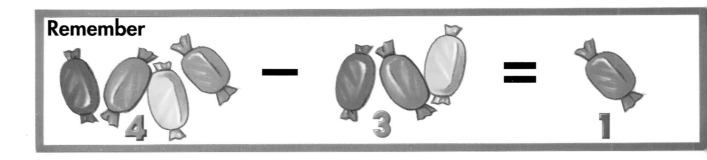

Try this

There are 5 leaves in this picture.

How many leaves fell from the tree? How many are still on the tree?

- How many birds are there? How many birds sitting on the branch? How many flew away?
- How many butterflies? Subtract the ones on the flower. It will tell you the number of butterflies flying.

Subtract on your own

Put your finger on the 9. Now count 4 balloons backward.
How many balloons are left?

1 2 3 4 5 6 7 8 9

What do we need subtraction for?

Subtraction helps us find out what is left when you take away a group of things.

When you pay for something, you know how much money you should get back.

The book costs 8 dollars. You pay with a 10 dollar bill. How many dollar bills should you get back in change?

Remember		
2 - 1 = 1	5 - 1 = 4	8 - 1 = 7
3 - 1 = 2	6 - 1 = 5	9 - 1 = 8
4 - 1 = 3	7 - 1 = 6	

Try this

- ▪ How many fish do you see in the picture?
- ▪ How many fish have been caught?
- ▪ How many fish are still in the water?

Subtract on your own

You eat at 6   and go to bed at 9.

How many hours
have gone by
since the time you
ate and the time
you went to bed?

How do we subtract?

We subtract by taking away.

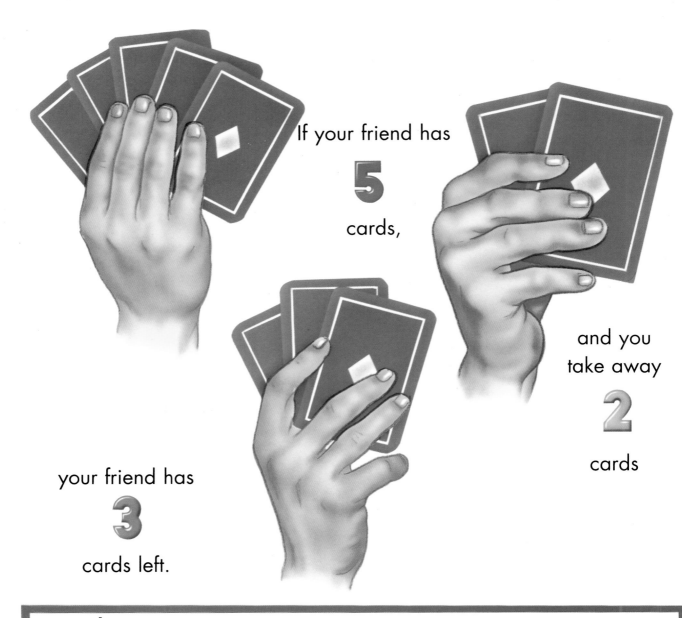

If your friend has **5** cards,

and you take away **2** cards

your friend has **3** cards left.

Remember		
3 - 2 = 1	6 - 2 = 4	9 - 2 = 7
4 - 2 = 2	7 - 2 = 5	
5 - 2 = 3	8 - 2 = 6	

Try this ■ How many sand castles do you see?
■ How many sand castles are still in one piece?

Subtract on your own.
Subtract. How many are left every time?

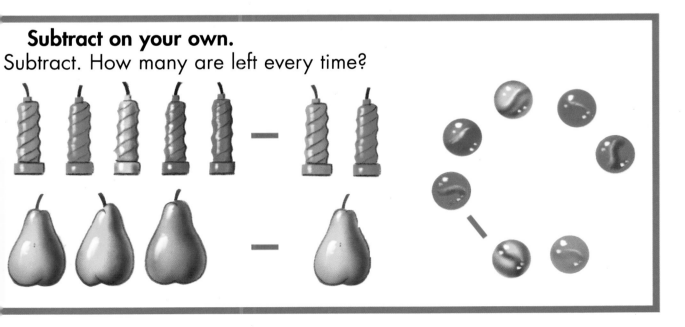

Index